Tenebrae in Aeternum

Benjamin Blake

Tenebrae in Aeternum

A Collection of Stygian Verse

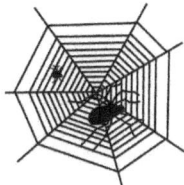

Hippocampus Press

New York

Published by Hippocampus Press
P.O. Box 641, New York, NY 10156.
www.hippocampuspress.com

Cover star: Lola Zaza Crowley (1907–1990), daughter of Aleister Crowley. Photograph attributed to Aleister Crowley. Cover design by Daniel V. Sauer, dansauerdesign.com.

Title page image: "Devil Making People Trample on Cross" from *Compendium Maleficarum,* by Francesco Maria Guazzo, 1608. Hippocampus Press logo by Anastasia Damianakos.

"Mayflowers" and "Chimerical" first appeared in *CultureCult Magazine* (India).

First Edition
1 3 5 7 9 8 6 4 2

ISBN 978-1-61498-313-2 paperback
ISBN 978-1-61498-315-6 ebook

Contents

Introduction

Benjamin Blake is one of the most bracing voices in contemporary weird poetry. This new collection, following upon his scintillating first volume, *Standing on the Threshold of Madness* (2017), confirms that Blake's work, while diverse in theme, tone, and subject-matter, is nonetheless unified by vibrant, impressionistic imagery, a focus on the profoundest emotions—not merely fear and terror, but love, melancholy, heartbreak, and despair—afflicting the human race, and a deftness of expression that renders each of his poems a miniature exposé of human frailty.

One of the most compelling features of Blake's verse is its emphasis on the intermingled elements of love, sex, and death. Beyond such paeans to the *ewige weibliche* ("eternal feminine") that we find in "Phantasm" and "Succubus," we encounter the fusion of sex and death in "Stolen Hearse," "Lychgate," and "Test Strip." Particularly affecting is "The Charlotte Wheel," a long poem about "The wanting daughter / Of a lunatic father / And a blood-soaked wolf."

It will also be observed that many of Blake's poems include explicit religious—and usually Christian—imagery. This does not by any means indicate any religious orthodoxy on Blake's part; indeed, a poem such as "St. Catherine's," with its melding of Catholicism and Satanism, suggests the very reverse; as do the grim lines in "Winchester": "Your God is as useless / As paper houses / In a spring storm." I do not presume to know the particulars of Blake's religious sensibilities, but it becomes clear that, in a poem such as "Hades," the myth of hell is being used to underscore the endurance of the indomitable human spirit, just as in "Doom Painting" religious language is used to underscore images of universal cataclysm. "Jaguar" (a poem nominally about the automobile, not the animal) is, on the surface, merely a recital of a brutal Satanic ritual; but it features a deft turn to supernaturalism at the end. And who can forget the extraordinary lines in "Campanile": "Stigmata bleeding / Like a spilt bottle of Chianti"?

The bleak pessimism that we find in "The Nightmare Card" is reflected in many of Blake's poems. Consider the imperishable lines in "A Sunken Star": "Some people are nothing but tombs /

Filled with dried flesh and dust / Locked from the inside." "Theatre of War," with its cheerless depiction of the horrors of warfare, and "For Hope, Despair," with its poignant couplet ("The days will never be anything / Other than overcast"), convey the anti-natalism of Schopenhauer and Ligotti as pungently as can be imagined.

Although much of Blake's poetry is imagistic, he is not above producing miniature stories in verse. This is exactly what he does in "Ever So Faint," a compact haunted house tale, as well as "Black Lake Wolf." Ghosts, werewolves, vampires, and other standard creatures from myth and folklore are found throughout this book, but they are always put on display with novelty of approach and an awareness of the fundamentally human symbolism they embody.

A throwaway line in "Spent Shells" reads, "I remember a time when I actually felt something." This may or may not reflect the author's mood at the time he wrote this poem; but if anything is clear from this book, it is that Benjamin Blake feels many things, and feels them keenly; more to the point, he is able to transmute those feelings into poems of remarkable intensity and power, so that they permanently colour every reader's view of our fragile tenancy of this earth.

—S. T. JOSHI

Tenebrae in Aeternum

For no one

The nightingale has stopped singing

A Note on the Text

Don't try to decipher
The entrails offered
For only one knows the true meaning
And it isn't you

Overture

A crumbling cemetery
Nestled in sprawling woodlands
Stones stand crooked, strangled by ivy
Kissed by the pale December moonlight

The dead still of night
Broken by the piercing shriek of a barn owl
And the sound of desiccated leaves
Stirring underfoot

From the clearing's edge
Witch-hazel parts
And a tenebrous figure
Steps into the garden of the forgotten
The owl takes to silent wing
As clouds smother the heavens
And it begins

The Gates of Hell
Stand Open Once More

Welcome home

That short while was far too long

A forked tail is better than a forked tongue

And sharpened fangs

Greater than a mouthful of perfect fucking teeth

I'll take what is needed

Without a second thought or backward glance

This time the lesson is learnt for life:

Stand always in flames

Stab or be stabbed

And never tell the full truth

Crematorium

Coming home feels like a funeral
A solemn procession
Down streets paved with tombstone
A dirge droning through deserted churchyards
As the car rolls slowly through
A town forsaken by the common God

A choir of Catholic schoolgirls
Stand in the shadow of a monolithic bell-tower
The crucifixes they clutch to their pert chests
Have known damp caves of delirious sacrament

Coffin-nailed to the town hall's double doors
Flaps a love-letter to lost nights
As ash falls from the sky
Like flakes of winter snow
Settling on this obituary
Of a road map

A Prayer to Brother Bacchus

Reeling from red wine
I found a newfound feeling
And I think I may be immortal

Stumble down the front steps
Smoke tumbling from a smirking mouth
And a book of matches in the chest pocket

The night is too young to take advantage of
But the clock is ticking in the right direction
And the streetlamps are flickering in Morse-code-message
Coordinates to your bedroom floor

Goetic Demons in Popular Culture

The exorcism was botched
Now wine pisses like slit wrists
As crucifixes are used in creative fashions
And the dog tears a limb from a lost child's doll

Let's burn the church
The guests are growing bored of small talk
And there's nothing like the glow of cathedral coals
To take the edge off

Thrashing about the bed
Stained sheets tied around the wrists and ankles
She gives birth to something
Quite unnatural

Burning Coffins

This town is cursed
Half a name, and still kills
Some things can't be washed clean
With any amount of blood

She walks amongst burning boxes of pine
Wedding school dress
Soon engulfed in flame
As she sinks into a charring cavity
Forsaking future vows
That dissipated
Like paper flowers in cemetery rain

Dawn will soon come
Rendering the remaining soulless to ash
But only time will prove this purge's success
And for Them
That means nothing

I Am One with the
Dead Trees & Razorblade Winters

This tomb is much too cold

As all three-and-a-half hands point south

And the pages on the calendar

Curl up and die with the dead leaves

This mind has been fractured one too many times

Though I use the insanity to my advantage

Scrawling words on makeshift parchment

While watching buildings rise from the leaping flames

Old bones that grew disfigured

Now comfortable beneath atrophic skin

But the all-familiar thirst for blood

Never wanes

Never will

Est Scientia Dei

Stockinged legs
Slide out of a black cab
White blouse tight across the chest
Taking stone steps one at a time
Beneath the cross atop the entrance arch
That stands against a looming grey Midlands sky

Polite boredom in the classroom
As Sister Mary paces, strap poised
Unaware of a passing note
To meet in the courtyard behind the library come lunch

Pale hands
Place the board upon the paving stones
Fingertips reach for the ghost eye
As an icy wind sweeps through the schoolyard
Swirling leaves and rustling paper scraps
The planchette begins to move

Like Knives

Standing amongst burning leaves
As a pair of black cats
Entwine themselves around her sheered legs
And her dark hair falls
About her pallid face
In all its otherworldly glory

She speaks, her voice a graveyard whisper
Carried in the chill of the autumn night
And her fingers creep
Like spiders of porcelain
Right into my mouth

Lying down in doll's houses
Her limbs deliriously suffocating
And a full heart
That will never spill
Her enraptured secrets

Sycamores

Circle of trees
The rain falls heavy
A three-pronged symbol
Scratched in soil
Marked with stones
It only happens every forty years or so
The cloaked companions
Heads bowed before a still Goddess
Sometimes you have to kill the ones you love
For the greater good at hand

The Nightmare Card

Forever swallowing swords
Doesn't do much
To ease this nervous disposition
And the feeling of sickness
That swells in the pit of my stomach
Is threatening to burst its banks

Complete and utter hopelessness
Has become second nature
A fundamental part
Of this tortured being

And there's nowhere to go
But down

Funeral Attire

Small-town church
Filled near capacity
The priest with sunken eyes
And liver-spotted hands
Clutching a worn-out Bible

The casket is lined
With the whitest lilies
A single rose against the chest
Not a hair out of place
Her lips still haven't lost their charm

Hymns are sung
Between the stuttered and choked speeches
One final goodbye
Before the coffin sinks
To the waiting flames

Stolen Hearse

Catching glances from girls at funerals
Nothing quite coaxes copulation
Like the recently deceased

Sombre tones of speech and dress
I wondered if she was appropriately clothed
Where it counted

Huddled beneath a black umbrella
The rain came down hard
She pressed a swelling chest
Against my arm
And cried for some reason
That I wasn't familiar with

Anatomy of a Teenage Prostitute

Slice by tender slice
Razor-tipped kisses
From the neck
To desiccated wrist
Thighs ajar
With cruel intent
Wounded paw
Scratching at rosebud breasts
A copse of copper hair
Covers the burial mound of Venus
And her eyes
Hint at a life
Which once held hope

Carnal House

Humble servant
Polishing cathedral library brass
Curiosity piqued by certain leather-bound spines
That were carefully hidden beneath habit folds
Before continuing

O, child of God
What did you find
In those dust-choked volumes?

For later that day
When the light of the sun had all but faded
And you lay sprawled on your narrow cot
The Devil appeared
To whisper wanton thoughts
In that now-besmirched skull

Mayflowers

Loose-stemmed girls in summer dresses
Partaking in something quite extraordinary
As the dogs run rampant over croquet courts
And somewhere
A father wipes at a stray tear
Spilling down his greying cheek
With hands that won't seem to stop trembling

Jaguar

I.

Navigating narrow lanes
That wind through English countryside
Leather-gloved hands grip the wheel
Soon dusk will be upon him

The car steers into an opening in the hedgerow
Stops afore a tall iron gate, standing closed, between high brick
walls
The engine idles for a brief moment
Then the gates swing inward

He rolls up the long oak-lined drive
A solemn smile on his handsome face

Gravel crunches beneath the tires
As a vast and sprawling manor comes into sight
And the vehicle rolls to a stop
He cuts the engine, opens the driver's door
Steps out and strolls to the rear
Lifts the boot
And looks down at the girl who lies bound and gagged
His smile grows

II.

The front door swings open
He is greeted by a blanket of warmth
And a helping hand
With his ritualistic offering

The lobby is bustling with guests
Distinguished men in evening wear
Sipping from champagne flutes while making polite conversation
The nod and grin of approval
When he is welcomed by the Host

She is taken from his ward
And he is offered a drink
Asked how the drive up was
He starts to reply, when a bell is rung
The men stop what they are doing
And file into an adjacent room
They don ceremonial cloaks
And disappear one by one
Down a spiral staircase made of stone
The ritual will shortly begin

III.

A subterranean chamber
Lit by black candles
A pentagram is painted on the flagstone floor
The unnamed men stand in a circle
Hooded heads lowered
A gap is made, as a wooden table is wheeled in
And set in the symbol's centre
The girl is strapped to the heavy beech surface
And stripped of all clothing
The Host appears, as the men begin to chant

A serpentine dagger is held aloft
Before it is brought down hard
Straight through the heart

A tortured scream
As the blood pours out
Begins to pool beneath the table
The candles seem to dim
The chanting grows in volume

Somewhere, a large cymbal is struck repeatedly
The Host raises his arms to the ceiling
The men sink to their knees
The girl's stomach writhes, distends
The skin tearing as snakes spill out
Jet-black and slick as oil
They sliver through the pool of blood
Forked tongues darting rapacious

The Host retrieves the ceremonial blade
He dips his fingers in the gaping wound
Draws a three-pronged symbol
On the colder flesh of her forehead
The cymbal crashes like midnight thunder
The Latin recited grows almost fevered
She opens her eyes

Valentine for a Vixen

Dreaming of delicate days
Of a heart hidden away
In company of canines
Early morning cider smile
And the best legs this side of the English Channel

Lying in spring-time fields
A clandestine hand upon a stockinged thigh
Nuzzle close, my dearest dear,
While the echoes of the hunt
Fade away across the moors

Ever So Faint

The dilapidated house stands behind brick wall
And ivy-ensconced wrought iron
Thick woodland surrounds the sprawling property
Home to owl, wolf, and bat
Cupola with Cyclopean window
Rises from the crooked roof tiles
Cracked pane choked with dust
An opaque countenance appears
When the moon is just right
A young woman, dead many long years
Once flung from that very frame
Found splayed upon the courtyard's weathered stone
Neck bent unnatural and severe
A thin trickle of blood spilling from the corner of her pretty mouth
She can never leave those crumbling walls
Or so lore has it

The Isle

Harried witchcraft
I kissed my finger
With the tip of a razorblade
And bled into her name

At the makeshift altar
In the light of a stolen candle
I placed the Corazon card
Upon those two gorgeous syllables
And spoke words penned
In the richest red

The fire will come
The point of origin, the heart
And consume all
In its inescapable path

Pioneer Cemetery

Tombstones for eyes
The redwoods' roots twist through bone
Rabbit-warren insides
Inside a pine box
The Founding Father clasps his hands

Oh, my sweet Emily
Who buried you?
There's dirt beneath these coffin nails

A sexton brother-in-law
Buried in the very grave
He recently dug for a drowning

The feral cats relish warm blood
As I walk these forgotten avenues
Of the long-time dead

Dago Red

Drunk off an oversized bottle of Italian Merlot
I wandered the darkened streets in search of cigarettes
As the rain came down
Further obscuring vision

Fingers crossed
For a wine-soaked vision of the Virgin
Clinging to the shadows
Beneath the bridge

Yes, I am that troubled
Don't take it for granted
For one night
When the stars themselves
Have all but given up
I will find her
Waiting and wanting

And Jesus Wept . . .

Born at the witching hour
One midwinter night
Collector of bones and leaves
An observer of ghosts
Hung many years before
The animals are his only friends
Near-drowned in the baptismal font
The Chinese whispers of churchgoers
Admonishing: "he will put evil inside of you"
And I did

Glossolalia

The seventh daughter was found
Riven upon freshly fallen snow
She was not without her secrets
You can tell by the insides
And the tongues in which she recently spoke
Gave little coherent enough to decipher
A forewarning not heeded
That something was irrevocably amiss

The priest bathed her torn body
In a font of holy water
Where lilies floated silent
Beneath the frozen face of Jesus
Shadows cast from votive candles
Flickered across the chamber walls
And He wept tears of the purest red
As stigmata scars appeared on her cold palms
And she opened her eyes
For the briefest of moments
Before speaking these fateful words . . .

St. Catherine's

A churchyard at night
Young girls meander through the sunken stones
Stolen wine, secrets held
Just behind the teeth
A loose circle is formed
Beneath the heavy boughs of an old ash
Hands held soft in the pale moonlight
A faint glint off necklaces
As delicate chests rise and fall
(Inexperience can lead one astray
Unlock the latches on careful hearts)
The chorus of innocent voices
Rings out though the hallowed grounds
Eyes flicker to one another's
Half-smiles and stifled giggles
The Devil rises from the leaf-covered soil

Executing the Vivian Girls

They danced into my head in a watercolour dream
Petals of poppies laid afore naked feet
O, their intentions seemed pure of heart
I swear, I swear

The wooden frame of this narrow cot
Shook as vermillion poured from the walls
And Hands of Fire descended through the ceiling
Fingers poised, a dementia-crazed puppet master
Cavorting the Girls, in a fit of glorious death

The Western Front revealed their horns and true genitalia
A grotesque unveiling, amidst mortar blasts and screaming shrapnel
I couldn't be helped
The medic deserted this field of dying
So as the chorus giggled in delirium
I took my own life

Scissors

An empty house at night
A faint glow from an upstairs room
Leaves fall as you make your way across the sprawling yard
And carefully climb the front steps

The door swings open without a sound
Nothing but thick shadow
And the drip of a leaking tap
You step inside

Ascending the creaking stairs
You question the stains upon the walls
And where that god-awful smell
Does come from

Second-floor landing
Soft light spills from the room ahead
Slow footsteps, a quickening pulse
As you pause at the doorway
Before stepping in

A dollhouse sits
In the middle of the debris-cast floor
Its windows gently lit
Suddenly it bursts into flame
And a girl emerges from the darkness
At the edge of the room
A gaping hole where her stomach should be

She pulls a pair of kitchen scissors
From the frills of her dress

And smiles
As the bedroom door
Slams shut

Esoteric Symbolism

Markings found in woodland caves
Chiselled into the damp stone
Arcane promises of places waiting
Beyond the veil of this reality
Gleaned in the screech of wild-eyed owls
And translated in the tongue
Of visitors found in dreams
The threshold stands
Ready to be crossed
By those the unseen entities deem worthy
The others are vessels to be sunk
But only after new blood
Has been spilt
From a daughter's split lip
Or something much worse

The Charlotte Wheel

Seaside parks
A raven-haired girl
Limbs caught in fishing nets
Vivacious yet virtuous
Coquettish in talk of corsets
And photographs in swing-sets
Demonstrating the cheer squad routine
I was a king
On a throne of pale flesh

On second thought
She turned and ran
Throwing herself
Into my outstretched arms

Hiding beneath the cover
Of a cold stone bridge
The estuary awash with waves
The townsfolk cheering
As the stars
Were hung like thieves

I broke from the delicate hold
And turned to walk away
She stopped me with an outstretched hand
Not holding back
As she held me back

A short time passed
She grew full and blossomed

Those eyes
Cutting deeper than ever

A red dress
In an old house
A mind showing nascent signs of loss
The wanting daughter
Of a lunatic father
And a blood-soaked wolf

A kiss before a disappearing act
I caught up with her
In a small upstairs bedroom
Her soft breast in hand
I half lied
Until she broke down in tears
And banished me
To the relentless night

Years later
While smoking upon a park bench
I was approached by a woman ravaged by time
I didn't recognize her

Letter-Wrench

A stranger's house
Marked on the map in red ink
Waits on the otherside of town

This haphazard reality
Offers up the strangest of things

The mist drifts thick
Through the empty streets
Obfuscating its lopsided grotesqueries well

The door stands unlocked and unlatched
Opens with a faint creak
As you tentatively step inside

The walls sag waterstained
Sepia portraits obscured behind mildewed glass
An upturned shopping cart
Sits in the living room's centre
And from the shadows of the stretching hallway
Something begins to move

Dead Bird

The dreams won't stop
Shattered window glass
And heads turned sideways

The body of a dead bird
Decaying at my feet

She stutters shards of sentences
Sliced from conversations with dire outcomes
The pain comes fresh
With every syllable

The walls are coloured blood red
And her smile distends
Before her mouth opens
And past lives fall out

The car catches fire
Dismembered hands
Pressing against the rear windshield

Your mother never cried at my funeral
The raven takes flight

Pulsator

The sway of shapely hips
Down a hospital hall
Keep the convalescents entranced
And raise the heart-rate sky high
Those eyes maim
Slice like scalpels
Leaving no secret unexposed
The orchids upon the simple table
Do not near suffice
She will be the daydream death
Of us all

Circle of Salt

An empty roundabout, still spinning
The child disappeared into the surrounding woodlands, unseen
He was never seen alive again

The little girl
Found mauled and torn
Inside a salt circle
In those same shadowed trees

The gates of Hell
Guarded by the black hound
Lured to a death so innocent
By a smiling face and a gesture of the hand
There is no going back
There is no escaping
This quiet little town

Uncertain Death

The curtains closed
On a stage of weathered tombs
As the lighting flashed lightning
And the crash of a Chinese cymbal
Brought the boom of thunder
An actress lay
Face down upon the floorboard earth
Dead still and dying

The crowd applauds
The bloodthirsty roar of approval
None of them knowing
That they will never leave

Visage

A woman's face appears in the window glass
Vignetted in grime
The heart grows cold
Breath bated in morning lungs
And as suddenly as she came
She is gone
Leaving nothing
But a faint cloud of condensation
And a chill
In the marrow of my bones

A Sunken Star

There is a sadness around you
Something bleak and almost tangible
And these hands still shake
But your mind reeks
Of things better left unsaid

The fall wasn't enough
And you will live to regret
An existence so mundane and dull
That reflection won't ever come again
Even if willed

Some people are nothing but tombs
Filled with dried flesh and dust
And locked from the inside

Theatre of War

Traversing this field of landmines
Each and every day
Dodging bullets
And killing where I can

Home is nowhere to be found
And I'm beginning to know no other way
I'm afraid
That I'm losing my fear of death
That the blood that soaks these blackened trenches
Is what sustains me to go on
What have I become?
And is it more monster, or man?

The Grand Chancellor

Lost in the hallways of an old hotel
Worn carpet swirls underfoot
Patterns and symbols lurching in a drunken mind
A sickening feeling brewing deeper in the stomach
I can't remember the number of the room
Words were spoken at the bar
Ghost stories recounted over stiff drinks
That blonde kept a watchful eye
Cast over the rim of a glass of gin & tonic
Something hidden lay at the back of those emerald irises
Something that hinted at something larger
A strange fervour fell over these colder bones
Choked the heart out of the chest
Hands shook as I lit my last cigarette
When I looked up she was gone

Dead Night

I woke

The inexplicable knowledge an ocean around me—

My mother was dead in the other room

Cloaked in a pall of darkness

Hues of blacks and blues

As cold as I'd ever been

I felt all life leave the house

I would never sleep again

It, Too, Will Fade

Haunting the empty rooms
Of this century-old house
Reaching out to memories
Buried deep in the past
The animals are the only ones who can see me
Their stalwart company is preferred

Sepia photographs adorn the floral-papered walls
Women and men long dead, but nowhere to be found
At least, not in this realm

What is it that needs to be done?
So I, too, can leave this prosaic place?
The time is out of reach
And I sink further every year
Into a place I can't crawl out of

I know now, what I didn't then—
That death is not the end

Elderflower

Forgotten public park
Dilapidated swing-set
Sagging like a lopsided dream

Dead leaves scurry like small rodents
Across unkempt grass
As the autumn wind picks up

Faint laughter can be heard
From the surrounding shrubbery
And the crepuscular sky
Suddenly grows full dark

The wine's almost gone now
There are worse things than being alone
And the laughter's turned to screams

Lychgate

Seeking shelter beneath the lychgate
As the winter rain came down
Cold, and sharp as knives

Pressed close on the wooden bench
Ensconced in gaslamp shadow
I sought the warmer blood
Beneath the skin of her neck
And relished the swell of budding breasts
Beneath the folds of her blouse

She smiled, a stray strand of light
Caught fleeting in eyes
That betrayed a subtle hint
Of fear

She gasped and squirmed
As my hand sought a lusher Eden
Springing up, and dancing off
Amongst the tombstones
A naïve nymphet
That left me cursing
Beneath my breath

A Hole in the Ground

The still and awful quiet
Of moments before
Impending cataclysm
The damp of the empty football field
Spreads to the marrow of the bone
The leaves of surrounding trees
Seem to fall in slow motion
Before the ground itself
Opens up

The Sound of Reality Breaking

Television set stutters to static

It's raining glass from the ceiling

Where were you the day I cut my finger?

The blood somehow tasted sweeter

The walls are cast with silhouettes of dancing leaves

As I wait for the phone to ring

A young geisha upon a sprawling bed

Removes her kimono

Her eyes scream insanity

But her breasts are incontestable

I lit a fire inside my mouth

And now she burns like churches

I got lost somewhere else

And can't find my way back

Exposure

A photograph found in the glovebox
Showed a skinny blonde not-quite-smiling
Partially out-of-focus
And burnt at the edges

I couldn't remember what night it was
And her taste was already lost upon the tongue

Who am I
When I think these things?

Baphomet with a Broken Horn

She caught me off guard
As I stood smoking against the brick wall
Of a rundown liquor store

There was something wrong with her eyes
They saw straight through the mortal pall
And into the pale beyond

She left me with only a sly smile
And a sinking feeling
That it had only just begun . . .

Weepers

I've been giving her the evil eye
And dabbling in black magic missives
In hopes of a more glorious killing

Textbooks spell out desires
Better left unread
And those dreams that come at night
Hold the answers
To questions never dared asked
In the daylight hours

Lacklustre sister
Always standing in the way
With her bracelets and charms
And overzealous sense of morality

Meet me in the trees
There is darkness there
That will envelop completely

Amid plinthed busts of draped martyrs
And sycamores planted in crescent groves
It will come to pass
The passing of the sword and the cup
Brimming with the sweetest wine
Which flows from this sacrificial altar

Bedlam

The febrile ravings of a female lunatic
Barefooted upon the bed
As a desiccated nurse
Attempts to administer her daily medicine
And a small bird
Flies into the windowpane with a loud thump
Breaking its neck
On impact

Mr. Scarley

He comes in my dreams
Through bathroom mirrors
Of the heart
Pressing my body against the cold floor tile
He never asks why

He hides the knife
First blood not yet dry
And his smile is stuck
In my head for days

I was taken
As the stars hung themselves
From the ceiling fan
Spinning around and around and around
As I stared with wider eyes
And Mr. Scarley drove me home

Captivated

Secured fast by the appendages
Basement walls cold and indifferent
The sound of heavy footsteps
On the floorboards above
Dust spills from the cracks
No sound escapes
Parched screams fall short
Lacerations and loose teeth
The rattle of old chains
And the smell of new flesh
Rubbed raw at the wrists
The creak of a door opening
Now he's coming down the stairs
Eyes like an owl's
Pleading beneath the bare bulb hanging
As he shuffles across dirty concrete
A lupine smile
Playing across the face of your father

Vampirism

Forever on the prowl for demure maidens
Nursing some semblance of longing
A crack in the windowpane of the soul

Exsanguinated on the bedsheets
Drained of corporeal life
As silent as a moonless evening
And still warm to the chilled touch

Seeking refuge in the catacombs
When the deadly sunlight
Is due to spill over the blood-soaked horizon
Only to do it all again
Once subsequent dusk
Fades into night

Test Strip

Darkroom chemical hands
Fumbling for another's in the dark
And other parts of the anatomy
A little more intimate

Dead crows on cold stones
Fading into focus
As warmer flesh was tasted
And relished on lips
That smiled
For the first time

In the reddened light
Legs wrapped around my waist
And arms entwined about a neck
Etched with illicit kisses

A fire was ignited in my veins
That has never gone out
Even after all these years
That she's been dead

Fire Cleanses All

It starts with a spark
In the dead of night
Handwriting is soon engulfed in flame
A lock of hair
A ribbon once tied
Around a gift that used to mean something
Photographs are consumed
Peeling and curling to black
As my heart already has

A City, a Tomb

The city was buried
But still lives on
In some alternate reality
That occasionally bleeds into ours

Faces age sideways
Limbs emerge only half-formed
And new blood is somewhat incestuous
At very best

The heart, a graveyard
Nestled around a stone cathedral
The same dead natives
Rising to accost weary travellers
Who can never truly
Find their way home

What can one do
When they realize that the place they wish to escape from
Is actually where they belong?

Hades

I sank deeper into a Hell of my own making
Seemingly intent on self-immolation
I forsake my good judgment
If I possessed any in the first place
And danced with the demons
I should have exorcised
A long time ago

Even Purgatory looks good compared to this
But I will crawl my way
Back out of these infernal depths
Even if it takes an eternity

Campanile

The Sicilian sun beats down, unforgiving
As the priest stumbles to the bell tower door
Stigmata weeping
Like a spilt bottle of Chianti

The Father staggers up the worn stone steps
Hearing ghosts long dead
Whisper incessantly from the walls
Of secrets he thought no soul knew

A garbled, febrile prayer
Can be heard in the still of the arid air
Before a body throws itself
From an arched window

The bell begins to toll

An Older Hell

Sleepless nights
Stealing hours from the nightstand
This body withers a little more each winter
And leaves me thinking on the blade
If there is any blood left in these distressed veins
To even bleed out
It might make a small difference
If not:
There is always self-immolation

Cornicello

Host to sempiternal desires
This concupiscence only brings slight compunction
For I am as only as wanton
As the Devil who made me

These sylphlike maidens
Riven upon catafalque dosses
As the foxes whimper
A benighted benediction
And the moon hangs a deeper red
In a sky devoid of stars

These vinous crimes
Will secure a crossroads plot
But that which will come
From the woodland mist
Shall never be foretold

Recidivation

The recused
Still gormandizes between the easily pried thighs
Of recumbent milkmaids
Under the swollen moon of late August

An insatiable thirst for bloodshed
Spreading through the bucolic fields
Of Southern England

Vicars cross themselves off suspect lists
For a small crucifix was found inverted upon the tongue
Of one lost to this vicious animal

More wolf than man
He should have been thwarted
When the courts had their chance
But judges brought down simpler sentences
And the villagers didn't take heed
Of the widow's desperate pleas of:
"It will only get worse"

Bróðorlufu

Walking Old Country lanes
Drawn by henges
Enfolded in Stygian gloom

The hawthorn hides a secret love
Promised since faraway birth
And this wester hand
Is eager to accept

The clouds roll in
Smothering the dying sun
And sinking to torn knees
I worship pale limbs
In the centre of this ancient clearing
Build a fire of yew and ash
And read the signs in the skyward sparks
As I bathe in the warmth of the flames
And the ethereal glow
Of my newfound love

Swamp Thing

Sparse woodlands
Serving as a brief respite
From her creaking, clawed hands
And scathing serpent tongue

'Round and 'round she goes
Slowly sinking into bog
The marsh-water filling her lungs
Until it gurgles like a festering fountain
And she is transformed

The statuette of a serial killer
I placed on your mantel
Shall stay as a reminder
Of not what could have
But could have never been

Death Omens

The rats are my only friends
In this low, low place
We watch as the carrion birds
Swoop and caw outside the cell window
Debating whether the cadavers have it worse

A deep crimson
Rattled out of the faucet yesterday
I splashed a palmful on this pallid countenance
Before the copper tang
Seeped into my cracked tongue

Names and dates
Scratched into the stone of the wall
Most are unrecognised by this slitted eye
Though, there are a few . . .
One in particular
Scrawled with a fevered hand
And written backwards
Trailing off into damp nothing

Sometimes I still hear his cries

Phantasm

A wraithlike nymph
Upon the overgrown banks
Of the New Serpentine
A white dress, trimmed with lace
An innocent smile
Is betrayed by knowing eyes
But still I wander

I found her kneeling at the river's edge
Delicate hands dipped in a clear pool
When approaching, I noticed her horns
Petite and velvet-lined
Barely visible amidst her mane of dark hair

When she turned
My legs gave out
And I sank below the surface of the muddy soil
Amongst lost bones and broken souls
Descending into albescence

I woke
In a place I didn't recognise

Lucifuge

The birds took flight from crooked trees
And from somewhere came the pale laughter of young girls

The sky grew darker as storm clouds rolled in
And the foxes crept wry from their dens

It came from the smoke, the faintest of shapes
A vague glyph, familiar and omnipotent

The flames licked at my hand
A sign that I have the Devil on my side

The Forsaken

Descend the stairs into an earthen cellar
Where a coffin rests
Amongst spiderwebs and forgotten pieces of youth
Its mahogany lid will be heavy and reluctant to open
But it will

And you will stare down
Into a cavity devoid of a corpse
But more forgotten writings line the casket's bed
Than you have produced
In all your paltry years

An Attic, Sealed Like a Tomb

Rat-gnawed boxes of photographs
And dishonourable discharge papers
Sit beside portraits of past Fathers
Holding the same sly smiles for centuries

A once-spectacular mink coat
Now manged and motheaten
Hangs on a crooked stand
A letter, still sealed
Sitting in an inside pocket

Circular windows look out over an overgrown garden
Crumbling birdbaths and cherubs
Devoid of right arms

And somewhere, in the depths of this sprawling space
Rests a chest fashioned from yew
An ornate key protruding from the lock
Waiting patiently
For that someday fateful turn

Paper Skeletons

Ochre leaves scurry along the cracked sidewalk
As the darkened street lies empty
Sycamores stand shadowed and tall
Reaching crooked fingers
To a star-strewn sky
The bittersweet tang of being alone
The comfort in candy and cigarette smoke
The perpetual longing
For someone who will likely never come

But what was that behind a small window
On the second floor
Of a sprawling house across the street?
The faint stir of a curtain
A pale hand with slender fingers
A stray strand of blonde hair
It was probably just a ghost
On this night of all nights
The surprise
Would be small indeed

Like Flowers for the Dead

Oh, my lissom alyssum
Where has your madness gone?
You used to sway in winds of lunacy
And now you only wither

Somewhere, Something

Forever flirting with shadows
Trailing faint wisps of smoke
There are more than a few secrets
That I keep to myself
And nothing will change

Always whispering to painted walls
Wishing for the Ouija board to work
I know that you're out there sometime
And that I rarely make sense
Of this make-believe truth

Lucia

The cabin creaks in the night wind
As my heart strains at its confines
Somehow so alluring
With a delicate beauty
And a way with words, so haunting and surreal
This pen speaks what the tongue cannot
Articulates so fondly
The eloquence I yearn to share
And somewhere
The sun also rises
And paints a town in gilded light
The hands to countless clocks
Tick backwards in the future
The ring of nameless bells
Reverberate in the past
I for one
Have begun to dissipate
Into a sky of wayward swallows
Holding clandestine ribbons
In tiny beaks
O, blow fragile frozen kisses
And I shall try to catch them
Before I fall

Gravemarker

Another dead dog afternoon

A piece of childhood picked up and pocketed by the Devil

The first of the gang to die

His taste for blood will be sorely missed

And those late-night boxing matches

Paws and hackles up

Yellowed fangs bared to an indifferent moon

For all the women attacked on weekends away

And a loyalty that only the English know

My dear, troubled friend

Broken legged and lost of mind

Loved by few and feared by many

The lambs have finally stopped screaming

Phantom Breeze

Evening creeps
The jazz brush rattle of dead leaves
The strained death rattle
Of the summer slowly dying
And the sun sinks
Like a ghost ship
In sight of land

The stranger sounds
Of a stranger's lips
From behind a black veil
The witch hunt has ended
And my insides don't bleed
As they used to

Words are all I have
As I dance alone through darkened forests
Blowing kisses to the wolves
That wait just out of view

Some things I can relate to
Better than others

Chimerical

Stumbling into this diffused dream
Gilded rays of light
Caress forgotten skin
The forsaken do their time, naturally
And I have drowned myself in the fountain of youth
Many times over

Her lily-sweet breath
Expelled the water from my lungs
Those delicate fingers
Dressing wounds in clean bandages
And her lips pressed soft
Against the flesh of my cheek

Awoken to a nightmare
Laid bare upon cold stone
A heart beating in a clawed hand
And losing more blood by the second

The Oaks Are Turning Red

Autumn is creeping in
The rain-slick streets
Holding a certain familiar chill
The desk lamp is burning
And with pen in hand
And hand over heart
I shall bleed out
All that is home

Dog Rose

There was simply too much light
In those azure eyes
She left me wilting in the front garden
Alone
And desperate
For a swift and merciless death

Lake of Remembrance

Blood-red leaves fill the water
Along the avenue of oaks
Fallen soldiers, fallen lives
The war never really ends

The boatshed sits abandoned
Save for the nearby nests
Of jet-black coots
They show more humanity
Than their simian superiors

When the cold wind blows
Across the surface of the lake
I shiver in silence
Thankful for the dead
And finding comfort
In the irrefutable knowledge
That I will someday join them

Draped Urn

Early-morning walks in the local cemetery
To help ease the inchoate chaos
That swarms inside this troubled skull

My mother and hound understand
The beauty found near death

Holes in gravesite concrete
Filled with dead leaves and rabbit fur
The silence that speaks louder
Than the words etched in cold stone

The departed are all too familiar
With the misery bestowed upon
Those who stayed

Succubus

She comes in the night
In some small unwaking hour
When I lie entangled
In intangible dreaming

And she leaves
Just before dawn breaks
Imparting a faint pleasant scent
And the implicit knowledge
That her visit was sweet indeed

No Light

Oversexed and underslept
I keep a picture of someone else's wife in my wallet
You can tell by the hands
Shaking like a love-sick dog
Collecting leaves was once my only pastime

Percolated teeth, scrap-metal smile
The figure of an anorexic angel
Watches over this unmade bed
The clock stopped at six A.M.
But the rats continue to sing
And the rain comes down
And drips through the crooked ceiling

Where did I go?
On the night that you came around
I only remember the little things
And they're never enough

Soft Focus

A mansionette

Fringed with dawn mist

She wanders gravel paths bordered with Box hedging

Night-slip rippling against a slender body

As her fair hair billows in the chill of the breeze

The Beast grows his approval

Meretricious

It's always the eyes
Shooting messages like daggers
A visceral psychic telegram
Sent straight to the insides

Caught off-guard yet again
The SOS came too late
Leaving me to drown
In my own skin

Pen dead letters to living relatives
Kissing cousins and ex-wives
Exacting some small revenge
Served as cold as mortuary ice

Like an ouroboros
This bloodstained diary
Goes in circles

The end will never come

Cypress, Cedar, and Pine

Coffin lid wide open
Silken lining all but empty
Save for a few handfuls of loose, dark soil
In the basement of an old residence
On some quiet street
In an idyllic town
That doesn't suspect a thing

She sits in a simple wooden chair
Brushing her hair in an antique looking-glass
Lace nightgown clad
A small locket around a delicate neck
A faint breeze stirs the window's thin curtains
The mirror shows no reflection

The sun rises
Over the peaceful settlement
Citizens stretch and yawn
Begin to get ready for the new day
A mother climbs the stairs
To wake a late-sleeping daughter for school
Her screams can be heard from the curb

And beneath an unknown house
The creature sleeps

Viaticum

Last rites read on a deathbed shared
By man and wife alike
A priest in a plague mask
Reads from the blood-spattered pages
Of the Old Testament
And through the grime-thick window
Cloud-choked Heaven
Grows a little darker

The flesh of Christ upon the tongue
The dying stretch for miles
Stained sheets pulled to swollen necks
Beneath simple crucifixes
That won't repel a thing

The promise of pestilence was made good

Swarm

Swirling clouds of winged creatures
Twist high in the heavens
Above an ocean
That begs no forgiveness

I once lay with whores
Now I only burn

Radio towers
Sink into an infernal inferno
Children laugh, then turn their heads right around
Only the dogs are spared
They were already on the winning side

She once drowned a kitten
Only to pass the time
She now coughs up lungfuls of fetid blood
As the worms make their way
Through her convulsing body

Satan has come so far
We all knew him by other names

The end has no end

God's Half Acre

Wolves pace betwixt worn headstones
Impatiently waiting for their fill
As fevered girls dance to the drumbeat of death
Across the mausoleum floor
And the colder angels sigh with lovelorn eyes
That weep tears of the purest scarlet
The moon hangs full
A fang-yellow sickle
As sharp as guillotines on Sunday mornings
And with heavy hearts the children sing
Of blessings, exorcisms, and baptisms by water
Rueful is the waning night, for dawn will soon break
Like promises made on shotgun-wedding days
But when the late-afternoon light weakens and bleeds out
Dusk will come again

The Seasons Stutter

I battled through whatever it was that had come over me
(the foxglove obscured the face)
The rain came down hard
Relentless in its unknown mission
(I stopped dead in my tracks)
Water filled the empty street
Rising rapidly
Spilling over cracked gutters
And flooding front lawns
The sidewalks split
Formed tunnels straight south
(I lost my teeth in a pretty girl)
It stayed that way
For three whole days
Before the remnants
Of the summer sun
Made a final appearance

Meet Me in the Abyss

Sinking lower every second
I lost my tenuous grip on sanity
I think for good this time

I crouch at the feet of a pale saint
As serpents coil around perfect legs
And disappear beneath the folds of her white dress
And she smiles
As if she knows my secret

I don't deserve mercy
I chose the garden path
That led ever south

This city of the dead is vast
Suicide only serves
In sending one to a deeper level of Hell
There's no escaping
These high stone walls

There's no escaping any of this

Black Lake Wolf

An empty mansion
Ensconced in spring rain
Waiting for the glow of the moon
To fall upon the blackened roof-tile

An overgrown garden
Surrounds the tall walls
Cherubs hold small birds
In broken hands

The scant cemetery;
Stones huddled in a half-circle
Bear names and dates
Worn illegible by time

A figure hurries through the downpour
Hunched in a long overcoat
Up the front steps
And through the front door

The library is lit only by a single desk lamp
Surrounding shelves crammed tight
A portrait of a young lady hangs still
Before a knife is plunged through the canvas

Steeling himself amidst
The fluttering of moths
And the soft rattling of the spoon
Upon the absinthe glass
Tonight the moon is just right
And these hands will do
As they will

Maple Street Serenade

Housewives on Valium
Mouths open wide
Eyes turned to the ceiling
In prayer on the spotless floor
While outside the window
Orchids dance to a spring breeze

Medicine-cabinet smile
Teeth reflecting fallen stars
While the husband reaches a hand
Toward the stooped secretary
She finds a new use for the kitchen knife
And changes her underwear
For the third time that day

Behind curtained windows and closed doors
All along Maple Street
Dresser drawers are opened and closed
Bedspreads flattened out by manicured hands
Evidence washed away down the shower drain
Leaving nothing but a viscous residue
Clinging to the cracks
In the imported bathroom tiles

Husbands arrive home with evening
Pull black cars into still-warm driveways
Are greeted at front doors
With a kiss on the cheek
And a blade behind the back

The Killings Stopped

Teenage girls
Found with their throats slit
Upon the riverbank
One a month
For near half a year

No clues, no leads
No trace of evidence
Small-town windows shuttered tight
Strict curfews and even stricter parents
Still the bodies came

Then one day
They stopped
Leaving nothing but silence
And holes in the hearts
Of those who had lost
The smiling faces
Of innocent daughters

Winchester

An elaborate plot
Dense woodlands in fall
The hunter becomes the hunted

As he stalks the deer
I shall stalk him
Breath vapor in the chill of the air
Before a shot rings out
And a fine blood-mist
Hangs for but a second
After he sinks to his knees

And the faithful whore
Will pray
For the felled prey

Your God is as useless
As paper houses
In a spring storm

Pride of the Hometown

The old lady robbed
By those she offered alms
In that small park
Where the burgeoning rapist
First forced himself upon a child

Storefronts up in smoke
Flames leaping out of their busted windows
Left blackened and gutted
Like most upon the street
They had sat empty for years

The one roadside attraction
A derelict mansionette
Where a father slaughtered his family
Before turning the gun on himself

Spent Shells

A girl asunder upon the winter snow

As the wolves watch with bated breath

And the drinks go down

Like the sun over a dying village

That time and history will forget

As husbands are picked up by other men

On cliff-sides on colder nights

And dogs crawl beneath houses to die alone

I remember a time when I actually felt something

The Lost Art of Getting Lost

Sleepless mornings
Spent wandering small-town streets
Alone, and holding scant hope
To meet another
Like your own

The leaves of ancient oaks
Pirouette in the chill of the autumn air
Settling in quiet corners
Undiscovered by most
But hinting at an older power

We've forgotten what it means to get lost
In our own heads
And hearts

Autumn Harvest/Samhain

I saw October in
With hound and feline at side
Huddled together on the same worn blanket

Come morning
The sky hung overcast
Scraps of burnt Bible pages
Lay scattered across the park
A new pine box rested upon stone

The townsfolk were nowhere to be found

A Modern Life Cut Short

We need more wars and cigarettes smokers
Bubonic plague cases and serial rapists
Knife-wielding madmen holding blades to housewives' necks
As the family dog is put down for good
And little wide-eyed children watch on in horror
And maybe then we can forget about the slight misgivings
The obsession of body over mind
The witch hunts and public executions
The inane and petty problems of the modern man

Death should always be at the fingertips
Then and only then
Can we breathe a sigh of relief
And really learn to live

Kill Me

Slow seeping insanity
Sleeping more or less
Chain-smoking the nights away
Awash with the same old thoughts

Teenage angst has become the cliché
Everyone always wanted it to be
And thoughts of suicide
The new Sunday rosary
With a noose instead of beads
And hands that can't follow through

Brought back from the brink of despair
Only to wish for darker things
If there is only one way out
Then none of this really matters anyway

The Otherside of Suicide

Cigarette smoke and the aroma of black coffee
The calmness of early morning cemeteries
Of half-asleep dogs
And cats stretching

Late-night exsanguination
Newly stabbed best friend's ex-wives
The girl next door on her knees
Bound, and gagging for more

Daytime drinking by the town creek
Getting lost in old books and brown eyes
Rose gardens watched over
By stoic stone angels

Jail cell years eternal
A slow knife in the stomach
Stillborn babies
Born in wedlock

Your first kiss

Your mother's funeral

No one alive
You once knew

Sexton

I stand vigil
Over these past lives
Keeping a wary eye
On the dead
Making sure they stay that way
And disarming potential graverobbers
Of long-handled shovels

A-tisket, a-tasket
My once-love's in a casket
And I intend to keep her there

Death blossoms like a night flower
Fertilized with formaldehyde
Its fetid scent unmistakable
And hard to get out of one's clothing

Ashes scatter like ill-behaved children
As funeralgoers slow-dance
To another solemn dirge
And the tardy vicar
Spends his frustration
From the cover of the reredos

God has always been absent from our hearts
While the Devil makes himself at home

With Gnarled Hands

There's blood beneath these fingernails
And I can't remember where it came from
No matter how hard I try

The Patron Saint of the Sepulchre

Oh, how they weep
Angels with missing limbs
Missing the days
When He was still around

A crown of thorns
Now ever-so-delicately placed
On the bobbing head
Of a whore

The fonts were filled with blood
St. Michael's medal is submerged
And hung around the neck
Of the most unfaithful servant

Stained-glass memories
Of the most divine of sins
Committed in the wee hours
Of Sunday morning

Who placed the ceremonial knife
In the girl-child's hand?
As the Chosen fell limp
The Devil rode out
One final time

Only a Lifetime to Go

Serving a sentence
Handed down by forefathers born blind
Rattling rusted bars
As simpleminded guards
Pace the piss-stained halls
Ever eager
To issue a good old-fashioned
Brutalizing

There's little space left
Upon the stone cell walls
For further marks
Etched with blunted butter knives

If one seeks immorality
Then it can easily be achieved
With a life like this

Under a Blood-Red Sky, I Weep

The fire burns in the centre of the banque
Watched over by the severed heads of barn owls
And the ever-astute eye of the Firekeeper
A stranger in a strange land
I do my best to survive

The Guardian stands with talons poised
Ever patient, waiting for something to go wrong
Let's hope he never wakes up

The Ancestors walked beside me
As I brought home the clan-bird offering
I placed a hawk feather in the soil beneath the caves
As an unseen goodbye

The sky filled with blood on the morning I left

What Happens When the Firekeeper Fails?

The ravens croak out ugly cries
Take wing from the old oak
As black smoke billows
Across the morning sun

Dead grass is consumed
Swept through with dancing flames
Frightened creatures scurry for safety
Soon some will be but charred bones

When orange-suffused night falls
She will fall to scarred knees
And open her fanged maw
To be kissed on the mouth
By fire

Slashing Wrists with Stained-Glass

Cemetery stone

Crooked church in fall

Flames from burning witches

Keep fond memories warm

Conflagration congregation

The consummation of an already-dying marriage

This infernal inferno

Will consume all in time

While God throws his bearded head back

And laughs

Black Adepts

Invoking the infernal depths
This dark brotherhood never fails
Shunned by those who spread benevolence
Though they are the first to admit
The true power we do wield

My fellow Brothers of the Shadow
Void of corporeal husks
The damned Dugpas of the so-called Occultists
Our fevered time
Is drawing near

Son of Serpents

Deicidal tendencies
Developed at an early age
Pentagrams painted upon the nursery walls
In the richest red around

At the age of five
He disembowelled a neighbourhood cat
And hung the viscera in the local church

A little older now
He forced himself upon the preacher's only daughter
Holding her down between the stones of the Founding Fathers
As the other children attended Sunday school
With eager obeisance

The teenage years are always the sweetest
And it was here that he conceived what would become his
masterpiece:
The death of God himself

Perdition

Descend the nine circles
Head hung in a burnoose
A reluctant penitent
Who proved his paltry worth

A forest of suicides
Swaying in the fetid breeze
No matter how deep the dagger rends
There is never lasting relief

Lost in the sprawling City of Dis
A wayward angel on her knees
Reddened wings clipped, hair matted against a weeping scalp
She is ravished by a score of concupiscent demons

And yet, it is He who hath forsaken us
Signed the warrant of neverending death
And condemned our poor souls
To drown in lakes of fire
Forevermore

Doom Painting

Brimstone and burning churches
The stars fall like summer rain
As the damned spill from the mouth of Hell
Like so many armies
Of the already dead

Lucifer bows for one more kiss
As flames spurt from sewer grates
Searing flesh
And rendering onlookers to ashes

The Great Whore
Strips bone like bark
And in the belly of the Beast
Legion bastard children
Scream in vain for mothers
That lay slaughtered upon the glowing coals
Scattered across a scorched Eden

Lake of Fire
Spilling into an ocean
Tsunamis of molten waves
Washing over coastal cities
Erasing the sloven-hooved
And enslaving souls
Tarnished with immortal sin

World's End
Is not nigh
It is now

Catherine Wheel

These lopsided limbs
Spell out a misshapen past
Transgressions still whispered
In plush parlour rooms
A knowing smile, a horrified gasp
Depending on the respective audience

O, but the town got its crooked justice!
Punished the dire devil
That put evil inside the choir girls
And robbed the hapless young men
Of the water of life

But even after I shuffle off this mortal coil
These sibilant tales will live on
Casting unease in sleepless heads
And striking fear
In the weakened hearts
Of those who venture out
After dark

For Hope, Despair

The years have all but completely slipped away
Unforgiving in what little they leave behind
It leaves one sinking further
Into the tomb of self

An empty room
Devoid of human touch
Malnourished, and barely surviving
Off the memories of summer dresses
The smell of freshly washed hair
The first taste of burgeoning spring
In a woodland vast with possibilities

The nightingale has stopped singing
Only in dreams
Can a semblance of hope be retrieved
Swiftly dissipating
As the bitter morning chokes it back
The days will never be anything
Other than overcast

Until the moment of release
The sweet kiss of death on a withered mouth
Expelling what little life
Is left
In these blackened lungs

Necrology

A candle flame dimming
Leatherbound volumes line the walls of a stately study
The man sits hunched over a heavy oak desk
His life's work will soon be done

Dark dances with the Devil
Chronicled in esoteric verse
Maidens deflowered, the dead left behind
And other ill-gotten gains
Of the mind and the flesh

Come morning
He will be found dead
Just remains of charred bones
In a slow-smoking pile
Where a manor house once stood

The Missing Tower

My life's work meant nothing
Opening the steamer trunk is always a bad idea
An ossuary of undead bones
In which nothing ever completely dies

Death blossoms in the graveyard of the mind
Where white-laced girls wander lost
Forever in search of missing kittens
That cannot ever be found

Fall asleep on a catafalque bed of dying roses
And wait for the coming resurrection
There will always be new epitaphs
To carve in polished marble

Strange, the Way
the Sentences Seem to Scatter Like
Boneyard Leaves in the October Wind

The tree branches beckon with crooked fingers
As the streetlamps bleed through the palms of their gnarled hands
And the stars hang swollen
In the erubescent sky

My vespertine vixen never showed
And all the words went to waste

Step out into the burgeoning night
The chill in the air a catharsis
Sometimes, you need to leave home behind

Threnody

Melancholia, sing to me in a minor key
Of lilies placed on cherrywood
And a body that rests in the sweetest slumber

Of thuribles in churchyard mist
And dark-coloured dogs
That wait restless in the corner of the eye

Of handfuls of fresh soil
Seeping through the pale fingers
Of an hourglass figure

Sing to me of sycamores
That sway in autumnal breeze
Of wild cats tearing tender skin
And rivulets of crimson
Running down a soft white cheek

Melancholia, sing to me
Of the great misadventure
We call death

Benjamin Blake was born in July 1985 and grew up in the small town of Eltham, New Zealand. He is the author of the novel *The Devil's Children* and the poetry/prose collections *Southpaw Nights* and *Standing on the Threshold of Madness*. His current whereabouts are known to only a select few.

www.ingramcontent.com/pod-product-compliance
Lightning Source LLC
Chambersburg PA
CBHW020911090426
42736CB00008B/576